# Reasons to impeach Trump

NICHOLAS MARS

ISBN:
978-1-387-08761-7

# DEDICATION

I dedicate this book to my father who helped me see the truth in politics. I also dedicate this to my best friend Lana who has been with me through thick and thin.

# CONTENTS

|  | Acknowledgments | i |
|---|---|---|
| 1 | Taxes | 10 |
| 2 | Mental Health | 31 |
| 3 | Racism | 53 |
| 4 | Behavior | 72 |
| 5 | Russia | 89 |
| 6 | The Election | 117 |
| 7 | Corruption | 138 |
| 8 | Twitter | 161 |
| 9 | North Korea | 183 |
| 10 | Travel Ban | 211 |

# ACKNOWLEDGMENTS

CNN and Fox News

# CHAPTER 1: TAXES

REASONS TO IMPEACH TRUMP

# REASONS TO IMPEACH TRUMP

REASONS TO IMPEACH TRUMP

REASONS TO IMPEACH TRUMP

REASONS TO IMPEACH TRUMP

REASONS TO IMPEACH TRUMP

# CHAPTER 2: MENTAL HEALTH

REASONS TO IMPEACH TRUMP

REASONS TO IMPEACH TRUMP

REASONS TO IMPEACH TRUMP

REASONS TO IMPEACH TRUMP

44

# CHAPTER 3: RACISM

.

REASONS TO IMPEACH TRUMP

# CHAPTER 4: BEHAVIOR

REASONS TO IMPEACH TRUMP

74

# CHAPTER 5: RUSSIA

# CHAPTER 6: THE ELECTION

# CHAPTER 7: CORRUPTION

REASONS TO IMPEACH TRUMP

# CHAPTER 8: TWITTER

REASONS TO IMPEACH TRUMP

.

REASONS TO IMPEACH TRUMP

# CHAPTER 9: NORTH KOREA

# CHAPTER 10: TRAVEL BAN

# ABOUT THE AUTHOR

Written by a young high school boy from Los Angeles. He is skilled in writing and very knowledgeable in politics.

www.ingramcontent.com/pod-product-compliance
Lightning Source LLC
Chambersburg PA
CBHW030003190526
45157CB00014B/408